CELEBRITY BIOS

Prince William

Kristin McCracken

HIGH
interest
books

Children's Press
A Division of Scholastic Inc.
New York / Toronto / London / Auckland / Sydney
Mexico City / New Delhi / Hong Kong
Danbury, Connecticut

To Stacey and Fred and their little prince, Andrew

Book Design: Nelson Sa
Contributing Editor: Jennifer Ceaser
Photo Credits: Cover, pp. 4, 7, 9 © Globe Photos Inc.; pp. 10 Dave
Chancellor/Globe Photos Inc.; p. 14 © Corbis; pp. 17, 19, 20 © Globe Photos Inc.;
p. 23 © Dave Chancellor/Globe Photos Inc.; p. 25 © Globe Photos Inc.; p. 26 ©
Kevin Bruce/Globe Photos Inc.; p. 29 © Globe Photos Inc.; p. 31 © Karwai
Tang/Alpha/Globe Photos Inc.; p.32 © Dave Chancellor/Globe Photos Inc.; p. 35
© Alpha/Globe Photos Inc.; p. 38 © Dave Benett/Alpha/Globe Photos Inc.; p.41
© Dave Chancellor/Globe Photos Inc.

Library of Congress Cataloging-in-Publication Data

McCracken, Kristin.
  Prince William / by Kristin McCracken.
    p. cm. – (Celebrity bios)
  Includes bibliographical references and index.
  Summary: A biography of the young man who will one day be king of Great
    Britain, describing his background, interests, and how he has dealt with his
    parents' divorce and his mother's tragic death.
  ISBN 0-516-23325-4 (lib. bdg.) – ISBN 0-516-23525-7 (pbk.)
  1. William, Prince, grandson of Elizabeth II, Queen of Great Britain, 1982-
    -Juvenile literature. 2. Princes–Great Britain–Biography–Juvenile literature.
    [1. William, Prince, grandson of Elizabeth II, Queen of Great Britain, 1982-
    2. Princes.] I. Title. II. Series.

DA591.A45 W5555 2000
941.085'092–dc21
[B]
                                                          00-024227

CONTENTS

CHAPTER ONE

A Princely Beginning

"This is the first time a member of the royal family has been popular with teenagers. They see him as a regular boy growing up in Britain."
— royal family authority Jeremy Mark in *People*

Ask children what they plan to be when they grow up, and you'll get many answers: astronaut, athlete, firefighter, teacher, veterinarian. Most kids, though, can't predict what they will become.

This uncertainty is not true for William "Will" Windsor, Prince of England. This young man will grow up to be the King of England.

Prince William will someday become the King of England.

A PRINCE IS BORN

In July 1981, Prince Charles, the future king of England, married Diana Spencer, a nineteen-year-old kindergarten teacher. The wedding of Prince Charles and Lady Diana Spencer was the most-watched royal wedding of all time. It was broadcast live on television around the world.

The fairy-tale wedding turned Lady Diana into one of England's most popular and favorite princesses. People around the world also adored this new princess. She was young, beautiful, shy, and kind.

Within months of the wedding, there was even more reason to celebrate. Princess Diana and Prince Charles announced that they were expecting a child. Both Diana and Charles were excited about becoming parents. Fans of the royal family were excited, too.

On June 21, 1982, the world learned that Diana had given birth to a son. The name of the young prince was not announced for a week! Finally, word came from Buckingham Palace, the

Prince Charles and Princess Diana were thrilled to have a son.

Queen's home, that the child's full name was William Arthur Philip Louis. Before long, Prince William would be known affectionately as Wills, the nickname given to him by his mother.

A NEW KIND OF PRINCE

Thanks to Diana, William was a different kind of prince from the moment he was born. He was the first royal baby to be born in a hospital rather than in the palace. Diana had insisted on a hospital birth. Breaking centuries of tradition, William was the first prince of England to wear disposable, rather than cloth, diapers!

Charles and Diana realized that their son never could have a childhood like that of other boys. After all, William was born a prince, he lived in Kensington Palace, and he one day would be a king. The young family was so famous that it was impossible to go out in public without being surrounded by reporters and photographers. But William's parents decided to try to give their son as normal a life as possible.

Prince Charles holds young Will as the Queen mother looks on.

William (left) with younger brother Henry

After Will's birth, Diana and Charles still were expected to continue their duties as members of the royal family.

Did you know?
Prince William is left-handed.

These duties included travel to foreign countries. In the past, royal babies stayed at home with the nannies and servants. However, Diana thought that babies should be with their parents. She insisted that the family travel together, and little William was brought on many of these trips.

ANOTHER PRINCE

When William was about two years old, the royal family welcomed a new son. His name was Henry Charles Albert David, quickly shortened to Harry. At first, Diana was worried that Will would be jealous of his new little brother. Fortunately, that did not happen. Will loved holding Harry, and he was delighted to have a new playmate.

WHAT IS

There are leaders who are elected by the people
or political parties. There also are leaders who
inherit power or titles through their family's her-
itage. In Great Britain, there are both kinds of
government. One exists to make laws, and the
other exists as part of the country's tradition and
history.

On one side, there is a prime minister, elected
by the public, who has a role similar to that of
the president of the United States. The prime
minister makes important decisions that affect
the people of Great Britain. Great Britain is a
group of countries in Europe (England, Wales,
Scotland, and Northern Ireland) that share the
same government.

The prime minister works with a group of
elected officials called Parliament. Parliament
functions as the United States Congress does to
create and enforce laws for the country.

On the other side is the monarchy system.
Many centuries ago, all countries were run by
monarchies, which meant that one family or person (usually the king or queen) would decide all

A MONARCHY?

the laws of the land. There were no elections to decide who would be ruler. Instead, when one king or queen died, his or her title, money, and power would be passed down to a son, daughter, or a younger sibling. The titles would stay within a family until there were no more heirs to continue the family line.

In Great Britain, the Windsor family is the monarchy now in power. Queen Elizabeth II is head of the Windsor family. She lives in Buckingham Palace with her husband, Prince Philip. When Queen Elizabeth dies, her power and title will be passed to Prince Charles, her firstborn son. In turn, Prince Charles will pass on the title to his oldest son, Prince William.

The British royal family no longer has the power to make laws. However, they do have other responsibilities. The royal family still consults with government leaders. They are expected to be role models for young people. The men serve their country in the British military and act as honorary commanders of the British forces.

CHAPTER TWO

Young William

"Will is sensitive, temperamental, and spoiled. He realizes that people defer to him, and, even at his age, he uses that."
— a royal source on young William

It was a tradition that children of royalty were taught at home by private tutors. They did not attend nursery schools with other children. Once again, Diana wanted something more normal for her sons. She thought that William needed to be in a place where he could make friends and learn to get along with other children.

Diana could see that her three-year-old son was behaving badly, and she thought that being around other children would help. Will was misbehaving in public, sticking out his tongue at royal events and grabbing other children's toys.

As a toddler, Will constantly misbehaved in public.

Soon, all of England had given Prince William the nickname "William the Terrible."

In 1985, Diana enrolled Will at Mrs. Mynor's Nursery School. The school was near the palace, and security was tight. Charles and Diana wrote letters to the English newspapers asking them to let their son attend school in peace. Of course, William's first day was hardly free of reporters. There were more than 150 photographers outside the school trying to take pictures of the young prince.

THE BASHER

Diana had hoped that William's wild behavior would be improved by attending school. Instead, William began to boss around his classmates. Then he started getting into fights with his classmates. Will soon earned a new nickname: "Billy the Basher."

Charles and Diana were very embarrassed by their son's reputation. They made several changes around the palace, including hiring a

Diana often was embarrassed by Will's bad behavior.

new nanny, who was very strict. They also refused to let Will get away with so much bad behavior. By the time William was five, he had turned into "a proper little gentleman," Diana told *People*.

PREP SCHOOL

In England, boys from wealthy families usually go to boarding schools at a young age. Boarding schools are different from regular schools. Instead of living at home and attending classes during the day, boarding-school students actually live on campus.

In the fall of 1990, when William was eight years old, his parents moved him to Ludgrove Preparatory School in the English countryside. He lived in a large room with five other boys and was kept busy with sports and schoolwork. The school taught him how to act like a proper English gentleman. William also learned to make friends. Eventually, he was named captain of both the rugby and hockey teams.

Diana takes Will to the dentist after a rugby accident at school.

A moment of joy for Will, even as his parents were divorcing.

TROUBLE AT HOME

When Diana sent Will off to boarding school, she was in tears. She still had Harry to care for at home, and she kept herself busy with charity work. But she missed William terribly and Will missed her, too. Students at Ludgrove were not allowed to call home often, and they could only go home for a few weekends each term.

Yet it may have been easier for William to be away from home. His parents' marriage was falling apart. Watching one's parents fight is hard for any child, but Will and Harry had the extra pressure of the whole world watching. Stories of Charles and Diana's disagreements often were published in the newspapers. The Ludgrove School tried to protect Will by keeping much of the gossip from him. However, it was impossible to shield him from all of the stories.

In December 1992, newspapers reported that Charles and Diana officially were separating. When Diana told William, he was not surprised.

Will told his mother, "I hope you will both be happier now." Charles and Diana finally divorced in August 1996, after fifteen years of marriage and two sons.

ON TO ETON

In 1995, when Will was thirteen, he graduated from Ludgrove Preparatory School. It was time for him to move into a school for older boys. Although he was not one of the smartest boys at Ludgrove, Will did well enough on his exams to have his choice of schools.

Will chose Eton College, the most famous boarding school in England. Eton is known for its tough academic standards. Students study difficult subjects, such as Latin and Chinese, but they also have more creative classes, including computers and cooking. Will knew he would have to work harder to succeed in his studies, but he was ready for the challenge.

Prince William begins school at Eton College.

NOT LIKE THE OTHER BOYS

At Eton, the boys were allowed to go into Windsor, the nearby town. Because the students all wore the same uniform, it was hard for people to recognize William. For the first time in his life, the young prince could walk in public without being singled out.

However, Prince William never could be truly alone. For Will's safety, the royal family assigned him a bodyguard. The bodyguard kept close watch on Will twenty-four hours a day, seven days a week. The guard lived with Will at school and traveled with the prince wherever he went. Additionally, Will had to wear an electronic bracelet, which helped the guard to keep track of Will's whereabouts. In fact, Will still wears it!

Prince William plays with his puppy at Eton College.

CHAPTER THREE

A Prince Grows Up

"Will's not over his mother —there are moments when he really misses her —but he's doing astonishingly well."
— a royal source in *YM*

In July 1997, Will and Harry spent what was to be their last vacation with their mother. They were with Diana and her boyfriend, Mohamed (Dodi) al-Fayed, at Dodi's beach house in the south of France.

The next month, the boys were at their grandmother's home in Balmoral, Scotland. On the evening of August 31, 1997, a car carrying Diana and Dodi crashed in a tunnel in Paris. Dodi died immediately and Diana did not survive the complicated surgery. Early the next morning, Charles told his sons the sad news that their mother had

Will and Harry were on vacation in Scotland when they learned about the death of their mother.

died. Will was just fifteen years old, and Harry only twelve, when they lost their mother.

Will and Harry's relationship grew closer than ever in the weeks after their mother's death. The brothers were together to comfort each other, and to remember happy times with their mother. Both boys were actively involved in a family committee that decided what kind of funeral Diana would have. Will insisted that invitations be sent to people who worked with Diana on charity events, and not just to "important" people.

THE WORLD REACTS

Television stations all over the world broadcast Diana's funeral. People mourned the loss of the beautiful princess. They also were worried about how her young sons would cope with the tragedy. The sight of Will and Harry walking with their father behind their mother's coffin was heartbreaking. A note from the boys was placed on top of the coffin, among the flowers. It simply read, "Mummy" (the British spelling of "mommy").

William, Harry, and Prince Charles walk by the thousands of bouquets placed outside Kensington Palace after Diana's death.

Because Diana and Charles had tried so hard to keep the boys out of the spotlight, people around the world had not seen many pictures of Will and Harry. During the funeral, however, the boys were being watched by millions of people—not only on the streets of London, but in homes around the world.

LIFE AFTER DIANA

After Diana's car accident, British reporters agreed to leave William and Harry alone. They agreed to photograph the boys only at official events, to which the press was invited. This rule has given the boys their privacy during their boarding-school years.

Although Will missed his mother very much, the normal routine at boarding school helped him to concentrate on other things besides her

Will and Harry help escort their mother's coffin at her funeral.

death. Will did well at Eton, where he scored top grades, rowed crew (a team that rows a racing boat), played rugby, and was cocaptain of the swim team. Will's swimming stroke is so strong that he recently was named one of Britain's top one hundred swimmers for his age in the 50-meter freestyle.

Will was chosen by his classmates to be a prefect, which is someone who enforces school rules. He also was a member of the Combined Cadet Force, the school's military training corps.

CHAPTER FOUR

From Student to Star

"He's rich, he's gorgeous, and he's a prince. What more do you need?"
— English teenage girl in *People*

When Will began to appear in the spotlight more often, young girls everywhere began to look at the young prince a bit differently. No longer a little boy, Will was taller than his father, and blond like his mother. His warm, shy smile and beautiful blue eyes made him an instant teen idol.

In November 1997, William attended a lunch party celebrating the fiftieth wedding anniversary of his grandparents, Queen Elizabeth and Prince Philip. Family members and security guards were amazed to find six hundred teenage girls outside the palace, screaming William's name. This kind of reaction usually is reserved for movie stars and rock singers!

As Will grew into a handsome young man, many teen magazines began featuring articles about the prince. Girls started sending him fan mail and Valentine's Day cards. Wherever he went on royal visits, mobs of adoring teenage girls would hand him teddy bears and flowers.

WILD WILL

At seventeen, Will started going to teen discos, where he would dance the night away with friends. He wasn't allowed to drink because he was underage, but he was caught smoking a cigarette. The tabloid (gossip) newspapers quickly jumped on the story, and soon it became a royal scandal.

Will's father, Charles, gave his son a talking-to. Then the Palace laid down a set of rules for the young prince to follow when he's out in public.

At seventeen years old, Will was becoming the object of many young girls' affections.

Will may attend clubs and discos if he obeys the following:

- No smoking, drinking alcohol, or drugs
- No kissing girls in public
- Arrive and leave with a bodyguard
- Get permission to attend parties and be home on time.

Will still goes to clubs, including some of London's hottest hangouts: Foxtrot Oscar and the K-Bar. He likes dancing to techno music, and two of his favorite groups are Prodigy and Massive Attack. Will usually hangs out with a large group of friends instead of going on a date. A close friend of Will's told *YM*, "Will doesn't really date. But he has girlfriends—he tends to like blondes who look a bit like Diana."

WILL'S STYLE

In addition to his blond good looks, William has inherited something else from his mother. He

Did you know?

When William becomes King of England, his face will appear on British money!

knows how to charm his fans. He doesn't run away from the young girls who swoon over him on the street. Instead, he often smiles, shakes their hands, and thanks them for the teddy bears and flowers they give him. "He's carried on what Diana was famous for—being natural and having a laugh," reporter Jane Kerr told *YM*.

Princess Diana also was known for her great sense of style. Apparently, Will has the same good taste as did his mother. *People* voted Will one of the "Best Dressed People of 1996" for his classic look. He's often photographed wearing clothing by American designers, such as Tommy Hilfiger and Ralph Lauren. Yet he's also created a sensation by wearing things considered inappropriate for the royal family. When he was spot-

Many people thought that Will's choice of eyewear was not appropriate for a member of the royal family.

ted wearing wraparound sunglasses, the English newspaper the *Daily Telegraph* called it "a fashion mistake."

ENTERING ADULTHOOD

Over the summer of 1999, William took one of the tests most important to a teenager—a driving test. He passed his exam with flying colors. Good thing, because Will was eager to drive his favorite birthday present from his father—a shiny new Volkswagen Golf! His personalized license plate reads WILLS 1.

William also had his first work experience that summer. He worked as an intern at Christie's, an art auction house. An auction house is a business where works of art and other valuables are bought and sold. Will has a great interest in art history, so the job was a good stepping-stone for him. Will has even mentioned a possible future as an art history professor or museum employee. Yet that summer, Will was treated just like any other intern. He worked from 9 A.M. to 5 P.M. typing, photocopying, filing, and even making tea for his coworkers!

WHAT'S NEXT?

After William graduated from Eton in 2000, he traveled overseas. He went to Belize, Chile, and several countries in Africa. His favorite activity, however, was working on a dairy farm in England. William got up at 4 A.M. to milk cows and do other chores. For his hard work, William was paid £3.20 (about $4.80) an hour!

In September 2001, William began his studies at the University of St. Andrews, in Scotland. There, he is studying Art History. William doesn't want to be treated differently from other students while in college. "I want to go there [St. Andrews] and be an ordinary student," he says.

However, William's future will certainly not be ordinary. Someday, Prince William will become King William V of England. Who will be his queen? There is no way to tell, but millions of young women around the world would love to apply for the job!

After he graduates from college, Prince William may decide to follow in his father's footsteps and serve in the military.

TIMELINE

1981 • Prince Charles marries Lady Diana Spencer.

1982 • Prince William is born.

1984 • Prince Harry is born.

1990 • Will enters Ludgrove Preparatory School.

1992 • Charles and Diana separate.

1995 • Will enters Eton.

1996 • Diana and Charles divorce.
Will is voted one of *People*'s "Best Dressed People of 1996."

1997 • Diana passes away.

1999 • Will works as an intern at Christie's.
Will gets a driver's license.

2000 • Will graduates from Eton.

2001 • Will enters University of St. Andrews, in Scotland.

FACT SHEET

Name	Prince William Arthur Philip Louis Windsor
Born	June 21, 1982
Birthplace	Paddington, London (England)
Family	Princess Diana (passed away August 31, 1997), Prince Charles, Prince Henry (known as Harry)
Hair	Sandy blond
Eyes	Blue
Height	6' 2"
Nicknames	Wills, Dreamboat Willy, His Royal Sighness
Pet	Widgeon, a black Labrador retriever
Car	VW Golf
Music	Techno and classical

Favorites

Bands	Pulp, Massive Attack, the Fugees, Oasis, Prodigy
Food	pasta, hamburgers, chocolate, fruit salad, venison (deer meat)
Drink	Coca-cola
Colors	blue, green
Movies	action-adventure
Books	science fiction, adventure
Sports	polo, rowing, rugby, skiing, soccer, swimming, tennis
Hobbies	acting in school plays, mountain biking, playing video games, drawing, painting
Subjects	art, biology, computers, geography, poetry

auction house a business where works of art and
   other valuables are bought and sold

Buckingham Palace the palace in London where
   Queen Elizabeth (William's grandmother)
   lives

crew a team that rows a racing boat

England an island country in Great Britain

government the members of a country or a soci-
   ety who make and enforce laws

Great Britain a group of countries (England,
   Wales, Scotland, and Northern Ireland) in
   Europe that share the same government

heir one to whom something is passed on
   (money, land, a title, etc.)

inherit to receive something passed on from
   another person (see heir)

intern a student working in a business to gain
   practical experience

NEW WORDS

Kensington Palace a palace in London where the Prince of Wales (Prince Charles) lives

monarchy a form of government in which a family or person makes all the rules and laws

nanny a person who cares for a child

parliament a group of elected officials that makes a country's laws

prime minister the official head of parliament

rugby an English sport that is a combination of American soccer and football

tabloid a gossip newspaper or magazine

throne a seat on which a king or queen sits; also can refer to a title or power owned by a person in charge

title a name, such as "King," "Queen," or "Prince," that indicates rank

FOR FURTHER READING

Buskin, Richard. *Prince William: Born to Be King*. New York: NAL Dutton, 1998.

Davies, Nicholas. *William: The Inside Story of the Man Who Will Be King*. New York: St. Martin's Press, 1999.

Degnen, Lisa. *Prince William: Prince of Hearts* (*Teen People* Presents). New York: Warner Books, 1998.

Garner, Valerie. *Prince William*. New York: Angle Publishing Company, 1998.

Morreale, Marie. *William: England's Prince of Hearts*. Kansas City, MO: Andrews & McMeel Publishing, 1998.

RESOURCES

WEB SITES

The British Monarchy
www.royal.gov.uk/family/wales.htm
Learn more about the royal family on this site, which contains pictures and information about Prince William, his background, and his interests.

Yahoo Royal Family News
http://headlines.yahoo.com/Full_Coverage/World/Royal_Family
This is Yahoo's official page about the royal family. It includes current and past news stories as well as links to other Web sites about Prince William.

INDEX

ABOUT THE AUTHOR

Kristin McCracken is an educator and writer living in New York City. Her favorite activities include seeing movies, plays, and the occasional star on the street.